This Lent,
might enga
Creation".
our relation
God who is
time, we ho
learning mo
have been given and building habits that last
beyond the season to protect and honour the
earth.

The daily actions suggested here – and the
reflections in the accompanying booklet for
grown-ups – provide you, your family and
your church with an opportunity to come
together to meet with God and rejoice in
the beauty of God's creation. There are so
many ways to be involved with this year's
#LiveLent. Why not download the free app,
get a group to pray together, or do some of the
activities as a family?

Many Christians use Lent as an opportunity
to give something up, to remember that
Christ went without during his time in the
wilderness. Perhaps you could consider giving
something up as well to help the environment:
maybe you could use less plastic, use less
water or save electricity by turning off lights.
If many of us do little things, they can add up
to make a big difference.

Archbishop Justin Welby &
Archbishop John Sentamu

#LiveLent: Care for God's Creation is the
Church of England's Lent Campaign for 2020.

The contents of this booklet (and the accompanying version for
adults) have been inspired and informed by the Archbishop of
Canterbury's Lent Book 2020, *Saying Yes to Life*, written by **Ruth
Valerio** of Tearfund and published by **SPCK**.

Church House Publishing would like to express our warmest
thanks to Ruth Valerio and to SPCK for allowing us to develop these
#LiveLent resources and we hope they will encourage many to go
on to read *Saying Yes to Life*.

Published 2019 by Church House Publishing
www.chpublishing.co.uk
Church House, Great Smith Street, London SW1P 3AZ

Copyright © The Archbishops' Council 2019.

Single copy ISBN 978 1 78140 173 6
Pack of 10 ISBN 978 1 78140 174 3
Pack of 50 ISBN 978 1 78140 175 0

This content of this booklet has been inspired and informed by
Saying Yes to Life: The Archbishop of Canterbury's Lent Book 2020
written by Ruth Valerio and published by SPCK,
which is copyright © 2019 Ruth Valerio.

Bible readings are taken from *The New Revised Standard Version
(Anglicized Edition)*, copyright © 1989, 1995 by the Division of
Christian Education of the National Council of the Churches of
Christ in the United States of America. All rights reserved.

The opinions expressed in this book do not necessarily reflect
the official policy of the Archbishops' Council or the
General Synod of the Church of England.

A catalogue record for this publication is available
from the British Library.

Design by www.penguinboy.net

Printed in Great Britain by Ashford Colour Press on
recycled paper made from 100% post-consumer waste.

How to use this booklet

There are 40 actions, one for each of the forty days in Lent, plus one for Easter Day.

For each week (starting on Sunday from Week 1 onwards) there is:

- A **theme**, based on the days of creation as described in Genesis Chapter 1
- A very short **passage from the Bible**
- A **prayer** for use throughout the week.

For each day (Monday to Saturday) there is a **theme** and a **challenge**. On some days there are suggestions of practical changes you and your family might take to help the environment. On others there are challenges to find out more about creation, to explore the Bible, to reflect and to pray.

How many challenges can *you* do?

There is also an accompanying booklet for grown-ups, *#LiveLent: Care for God's Creation*, which also includes daily readings and reflections, as well as a free app.

You can find links to all the print and digital resources for #LiveLent at:
www.churchofengland.org/livelent

From Ash Wednesday to Lent 1

BEGINNINGS

READ: Psalm 100

Make a joyful noise to the Lord, all the earth ... Know that the Lord is God. It is he that made us, and we are his ...

During Lent we prepare to celebrate Easter, when Jesus rose from the dead to bring new life and hope to the whole world. This week's challenges encourage us to remember that God created and cares for the whole world, and wants us to care for it, too.

PRAYER FOR THE WEEK

Thank you, God, for making this wonderful world. Be with us this Lent and help us to love you and to care for your creation. Amen.

Ash Wednesday to Lent 1
BEGINNINGS

Ash Wednesday
Give up something to help the environment

During Lent we remember that Jesus spent 40 days going without food and comfort in the wilderness. Could you give up something this Lent that would save electricity, plastic, waste or water?

Thursday
Thank God for making the world

The Bible shows us that God is not only concerned about the people he has made but about the whole of creation. Thank God for giving life to everyone and everything – perhaps find a hymn or a song to sing.

Friday
Pray for the needs of our world

Jesus began his work saying that he was sent "to bring good news to the poor". Christians are called to pray and work for a fairer world. This includes taking care to protect the life of the whole earth, including its animals and plants.

Weekend
Look after something living this weekend

Spend time planting some seeds, taking care of a pet or feeding the birds, remembering that God made and cares for all things.

9

LIGHT AND ENERGY

READ: Genesis 1.1–3

In the beginning ... darkness covered the face of the deep ... Then God said, "Let there be light"; and there was light.

Our reading reminds us that all light – and all life – comes from God. This week's actions help us think about how we use light and energy and how to make small differences that will help us and others.

PRAYER FOR THE WEEK

Thank you, God, for the light and energy that we use every day. May all countries act swiftly to reduce energy use and combat climate change. Help us to make small differences where we can. Amen.

Week 1
LIGHT AND ENERGY

Monday
Notice light around you

Sit and watch the sunlight, a lightbulb or a candle and think about the difference that light makes to our lives.

Tuesday
Make small changes

Little things add up to save a lot of energy. Turn lights off when you leave a room. Turn off chargers once mobile devices are charged.

Wednesday
Walk in the light

Walking or cycling – rather than driving – are good for our health and for the environment. Can you make one extra journey on foot, bike or scooter today?

Thursday
Let your light shine

Jesus calls us to share his light with the world. Can you suggest ways your family, school or church could take better care of creation?

Friday
Give thanks for light and warmth at home

Almost a billion more people now have electricity at home than did ten years ago. Thank God for this progress, and for your own home, too.

Weekend
Help those bringing hope

Read a webpage for a charity like Christian Aid or Tearfund. How do they help to bring light into dark situations, such as countries badly affected by climate change?

13

Week 2
WATER

READ: Psalm 65.9-13

You visit the earth and water it, you greatly enrich it; the river of God is full of water ...

Without water, there would be no life on earth. This week our challenges explore how we can use and enjoy this precious gift from God better.

PRAYER FOR THE WEEK

Creator God, we thank you for water to drink, cook, wash and clean and play with. We pray that everyone may learn to use water more wisely and share it fairly. Amen.

Week 2
WATER

Monday
Give thanks for water

Whenever you see or use water today, thank God for this amazing gift we often take for granted.

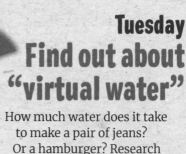

Tuesday
Find out about "virtual water"

How much water does it take to make a pair of jeans? Or a hamburger? Research online and share what you find.

Wednesday
Care for local waterways

Where are the canals, rivers, ponds or beaches in your area? Ask if your school, church or other local group could organize a clean up.

Thursday
Check your cupboards

With a parent or carer, go through your bathroom and kitchen cupboards. Could at least one or two products be switched for others with fewer harmful chemicals?

Friday
Don't give up hope

Pray for people already experiencing damaging climate change. Pray for them, and ask God to bring hope and courage to those trying to help them.

Weekend
Support a water charity

Find out about charities providing clean water and toilets in poor communities. Could your school or church raise money for their work with a bake sale?

Week 3
LAND AND PLANTS

READ: Genesis 1.9–13

The earth brought forth ... plants yielding seed of every kind, and trees of every kind ... And God saw that it was good.

Psalm 24 begins "The earth is the Lord's and all that fills it". This week we explore the trees and plants that fill the earth. Our challenges this week encourage us to do more to enjoy nature and to help protect it.

PRAYER FOR THE WEEK

Loving Father, we praise you for the beauty and plenty of nature. Help us to do all we can to protect plants and trees and to tread more gently on the earth. Amen.

Week 3
LAND AND PLANTS

Monday
Get in touch with nature

Spend time outside noticing any plants, trees and wildlife. Go for a walk. Get wet. Dig the earth.

Tuesday
Find out how trees help the planet

Trees do so much to support other life around them: people, animals and plants. Research the different ways they do this.

Wednesday
Save paper – and trees – today

Think of ways you, your class or your family could use less paper. Make sure you use both sides of the page and recycle all you can.

Thursday
Pray for people leading action on the environment

Pray for those who are working hard to encourage changes that will help to tackle climate change and conserve the natural world.

Friday
Prune your stuff

Sharing and re-using things is good for the environment. Do you have unwanted things like toys or games you could give to a friend, or donate to a charity shop?

Weekend
Remember to take a break!

This weekend includes Mothering Sunday, the half-way point in Lent. Enjoy a break and treat yourself (as well as those who care for you) this weekend!

Week 4
STARS AND SEASONS

READ: Psalm 104.1-4, 19-23

You have made the moon to mark the seasons; the sun knows its time for setting. You make darkness, and it is night, when all the animals of the forest come creeping out.

The movements of the sun, moon and stars divide our time into patterns of day and night, seasons and years. This week we explore how these patterns can help us draw closer to God and to the natural world.

PRAYER FOR THE WEEK

Heavenly Father, help us to know your loving presence with us through day and night, and in every season of our lives. Amen.

Week 4
STARS AND SEASONS

Monday
Start and end your day with a prayer

Jesus taught his followers to pray every day. When you wake up, ask God to bless your day. And thank God before you go to sleep.

Tuesday
Gaze at the night sky tonight

With a parent or carer, spend some time tonight (or on the next clear night) enjoying the wonder and beauty of the night sky.

Wednesday
Praise God for the wonders of creation

Look up the words of a hymn, worship song or psalm that praises God for creation. Perhaps you have sung one at a Harvest Festival?

24

Week 6
HUMANS AND OTHER ANIMALS

READ: Genesis 1.24–31

And God said, "Let the earth bring forth
living creatures of every kind …"
Then God said, "Let us make
humankind in our own image …"

In Holy Week – the last week of
Lent – we turn to humans and to the
other animals God has made and seen as
good. Our challenges are designed help us
care for other creatures and to remember
that every single person is special to God.

PRAYER FOR THE WEEK

Father, help us to follow your Son
Jesus in loving and serving
other people, and in caring for
the animals and the earth
you have entrusted to us.
Amen.

Week 6
HUMANS AND OTHER ANIMALS

Monday
Notice the animals around you

Count how many different creatures you encounter – pets, wildlife or farm animals – today and during this week.

Tuesday
Care for the animals who share our homes

God calls people to share in the work of caring for other creatures. Can you help feed or care for a pet – yours or a friend's – today?

Wednesday
Explore Bible stories featuring animals

The Bible shows us a God who loves and longs to save the whole world. Can you think of any Bible stories that feature animals?

Maundy Thursday
Be thankful for the food you eat

Today Christians remember
Jesus sharing a last meal
with his friends before he
died. Be thankful for the
meals you share and try not
to waste any of them.

Good Friday
Remember how Jesus suffered for the world

Spend some time remembering that
Jesus died on Good Friday.
And ask God to be close
to all those who are
suffering in the
world today.

Easter Eve
Write your own prayer for our world

After 40 days thinking about God's
creation, what do you want to pray for our
world? Why not write it down and share it?

Easter Day
CELEBRATE NEW LIFE

On Easter Day – and on every Sunday – Christians all over the world gather to remember that Jesus has died and risen again to bring peace between the whole world and God.

If you can, join your local church family in celebrating the new life and hope that Jesus' resurrection brings to the whole of creation.

Thursday
Notice the changing season

What signs of spring do you notice today?
Think of things you enjoy about the different
seasons and festivals of the year and thank
God for them.

Friday
Find out why darkness is good

God declares both day and
night to be good (Genesis 1).
Research out online why dark
skies are so important to so
many animals.

Weekend
Plant something this weekend

Plant some seeds or seedlings inside
or outside. Notice how they respond
to night and day and the coming of
spring in the weeks ahead.

25

CREATURES OF SEA AND SKY

READ: Genesis 1.20–23

And God said, "Let the waters bring forth swarms of living creatures, and let birds fly above the earth across the dome of the sky."

Our world is home to over 30,000 species of fish and 10,000 species of birds. God has filled the air and the seas with a dazzling variety of creatures and God sees that they are good.

PRAYER FOR THE WEEK

Lord of sea and sky, we bless you for the wonders of creation. May the people of the world act together to ensure the oceans and the air are protected rather than polluted. Amen.

Week 5
CREATURES OF SEA AND SKY

Monday
Explore the wonders of the deep!

Watch a nature documentary or research online to discover more about the life of our oceans – and thank God for the wonders of his creation.

Tuesday Can you use less plastic?

Too much plastic is ending up in the sea and endangering sea creatures big and small. Think of ways you and your family could use less.

Wednesday
Read about Jesus and the amazing catch of fish

Fish make plenty of appearances in the Bible. Read how Jesus helped Simon Peter and his friends make an unexpected catch of fish in Luke 5.4-11.

28

Thursday
Look at the birds of the air

Watch – and listen – out for birds today. Bigger cities and changes to farming mean there are many fewer than a few decades ago.

Friday
Feed the birds

Jesus tells us that God not only cares about every person but even the smallest sparrow. Can you put out some food and water for the birds today?

Weekend
Decorate some real eggs for Easter

Eggs remind us of new life and they play a big part in many Easter celebrations. Why not blow and paint some eggs this weekend?*

*Find out how at cofe.io/eggs